PIANO • VOCAL • GUITAR

# MAMMA MIA!
## HERE WE GO AGAIN

### THE MOVIE SOUNDTRACK FEATURING THE SONGS OF ABBA

T0195141

ISBN 978 1 5400-0320-8

Visit Hal Leonard Online at
**www.halleonard.com**

Contact Us:
**Hal Leonard**
7777 West Bluemound Road
Milwaukee, WI 53213
Email: info@halleonard.com

In Europe contact:
**Hal Leonard Europe Limited**
Distribution Centre, Newmarket Road
Bury St Edmunds, Suffolk, IP33 3YB
Email: info@halleonardeurope.com

In Australia contact:
**Hal Leonard Australia Pty. Ltd.**
4 Lentara Court
Cheltenham, Victoria, 3192 Australia
Email: info@halleonard.com.au

# ANDANTE, ANDANTE

Words and Music by BENNY ANDERSSON
and BJÖRN ULVAEUS

# ANGEL EYES

Words and Music by BENNY ANDERSSON
and BJÖRN ULVAEUS

*Recorded a half step lower*

# DANCING QUEEN

Words and Music by BENNY ANDERSSON,
BJÖRN ULVAEUS and STIG ANDERSON

# THE DAY BEFORE YOU CAME

Words and Music by BENNY ANDERSSON
and BJÖRN ULVAEUS

I must have left my house at eight be-cause I al-ways
must have lit my sec-ond cig-a-rette at half past
must have o-pened my front door at eight o'-clock or

do. My train, I'm cer-tain, left the sta-tion
two. And at the time I nev-er e-ven
so, and stopped a-long the way to buy some

just when it was due. __ I
no-ticed I was blue. __ I
Chi-nese food to go. __ I'm

must have read the morn-ing pa-pers, go-ing in-to town
must have kept on drag-ging through the busi-ness of the day
sure I had my din-ner watch-ing some-thing on T. V.

and hav-ing got-ten through the ed-i-to-ri-al, no doubt I must have
and with-out real-ly know-ing an-y-thing I hid a part of me a-
There's not a sin-gle ep-i-sode of House of Cards that I have failed

frowned. ___ I must have made my desk
way. ___ At six I must have left,
to see. I must have gone to bed

a-round a quar-ter af-ter nine ___
there's no ex-cep-tion to the rule. ___
a-round a quar-ter af-ter ten. ___

with
A
I

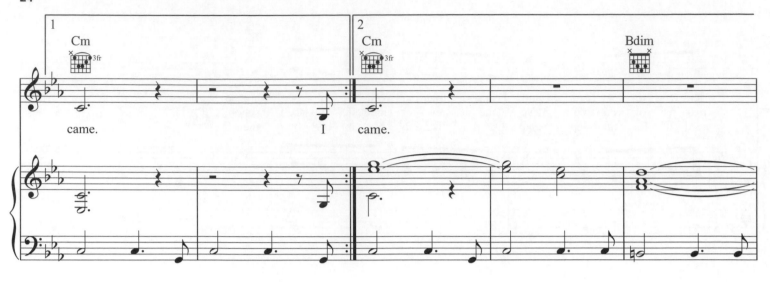

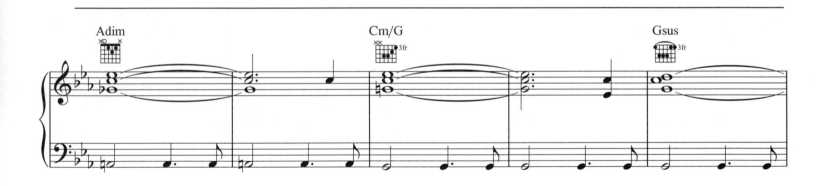

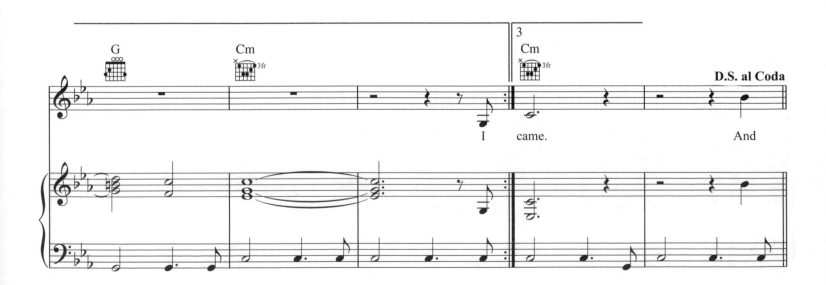

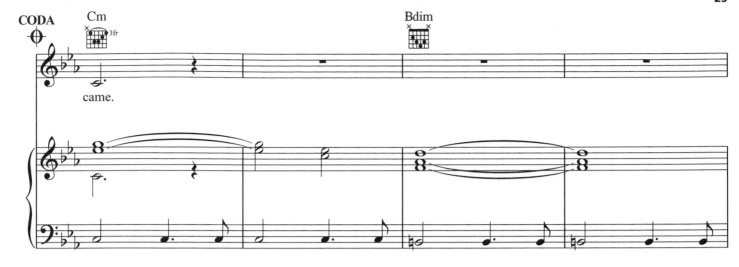

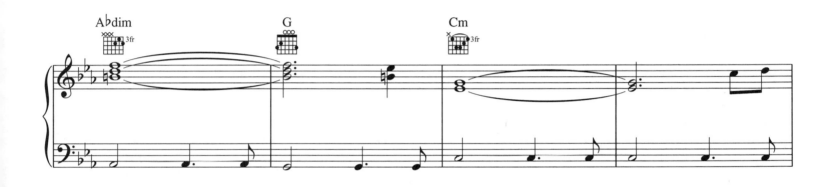

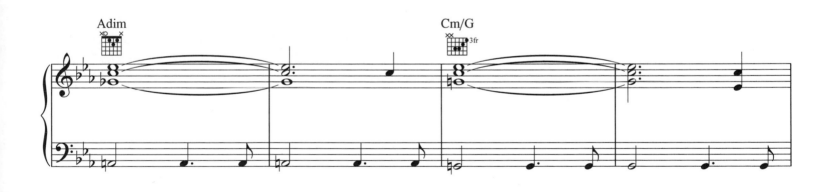

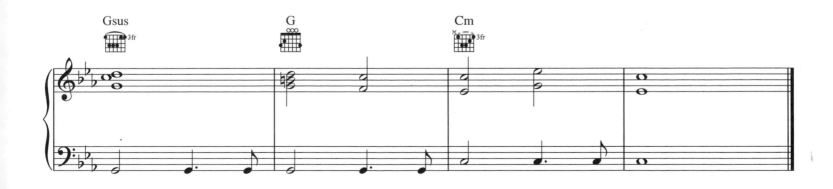

# FERNANDO

Words and Music by BENNY ANDERSSON,
BJÖRN ULVAEUS and STIG ANDERSON

Can you hear the drums, Fer -
They were clos - er now, Fer -
Now we're old and grey, Fer -

nan - do?
nan - do.
nan - do,

I re - mem - ber long a -
Ev - 'ry ho - ur, ev - 'ry
and since man - y years I

go an - oth - er star - ry night like this.
min - ute seemed to last e - ter - nal - ly.
have - n't seen a ri - fle in your hand.

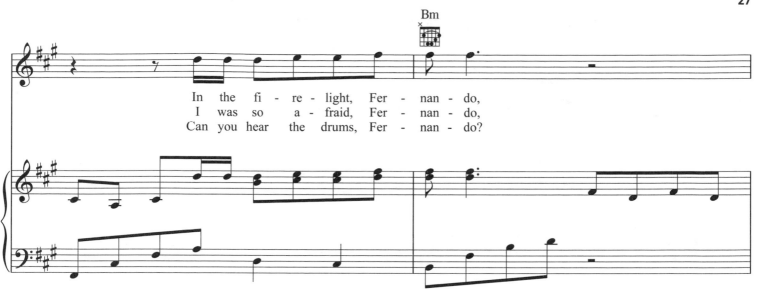

In the fi - re - light, Fer - nan - do,
I was so a - fraid, Fer - nan - do,
Can you hear the drums, Fer - nan - do?

you were hum - ming to your - self and soft - ly strum - ming your gui -
we were young and full of life and none of us pre - pared to
Do you still re - call the fright - ful night we crossed the Ri - o

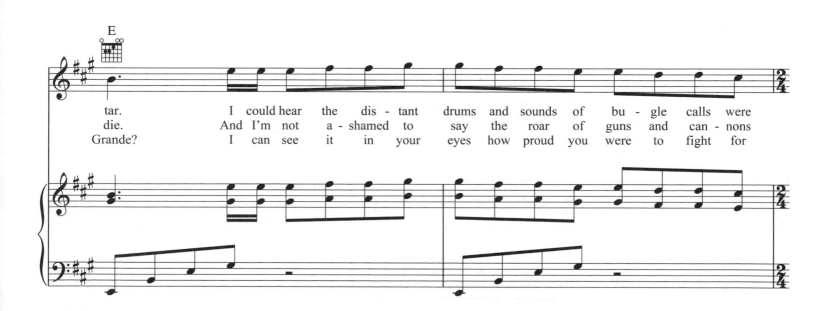

tar. I could hear the dis - tant drums and sounds of bu - gle calls were
die. And I'm not a - shamed to say the roar of guns and can - nons
Grande? I can see it in your eyes how proud you were to fight for

# I WONDER (DEPARTURE)

Words and Music by BENNY ANDERSSON,
BJÖRN ULVAEUS and STIG ANDERSON

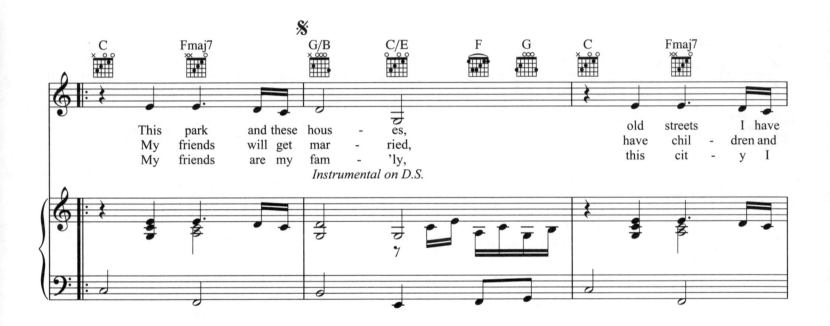

This park and these hous - es,
My friends will get mar - ried,
My friends are my fam - 'ly,

*Instrumental on D.S.*

old streets I have
have chil - dren and
this cit - y I

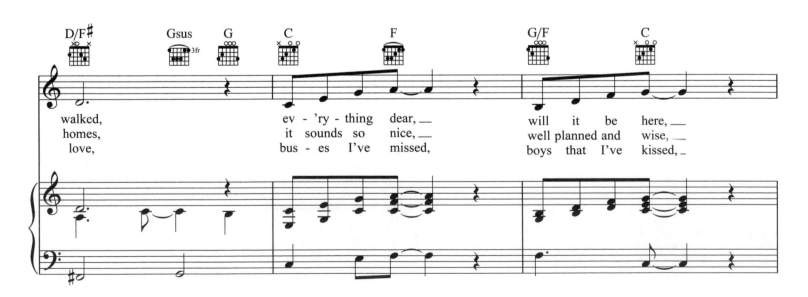

walked,
homes,
love,

ev - 'ry - thing dear, ___
it sounds so nice, ___
bus - es I've missed,

will it be here, ___
well planned and wise, ___
boys that I've kissed,

# I HAVE A DREAM

*Words and Music by BENNY ANDERSSON
and BJÖRN ULVAEUS*

# I'VE BEEN WAITING FOR YOU

Words and Music by BENNY ANDERSSON
and BJÖRN ULVAEUS

Moderately slow

I, I have known love be-fore; I thought it would no

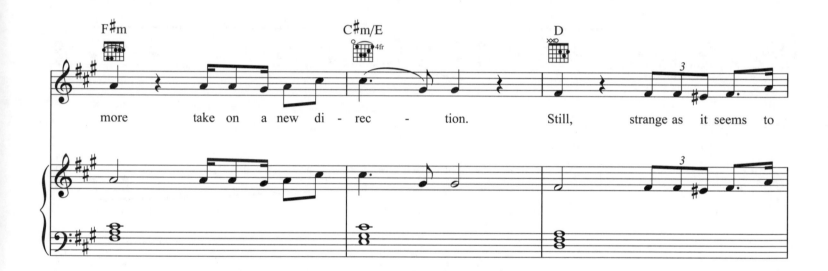

more take on a new di-rec - tion. Still, strange as it seems to

be, it's tru-ly new to me, that af-fec - tion.

# KISSES OF FIRE

Words and Music by BENNY ANDERSSON
and BJÖRN ULVAEUS

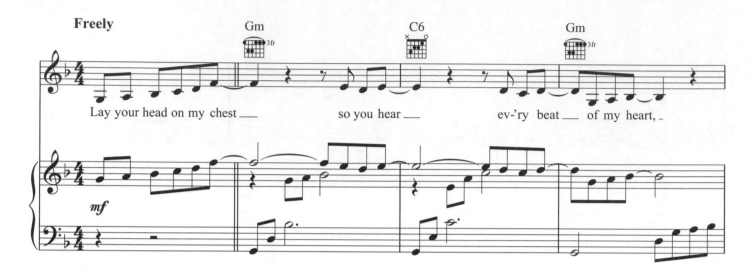

Lay your head on my chest __ so you hear __ ev'ry beat __ of my heart, __

now there's noth-ing at all __ that can keep __ us a - part. __

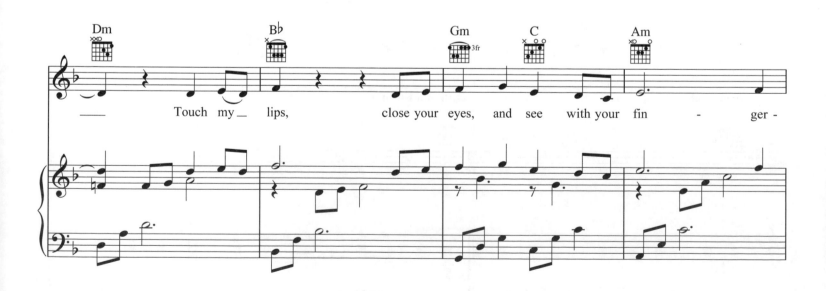

__ Touch my __ lips, close your eyes, and see with your fin - ger -

# KNOWING ME, KNOWING YOU

Words and Music by BENNY ANDERSSON,
BJÖRN ULVAEUS and STIG ANDERSON

Know-ing me, know-ing

do.

# MAMMA MIA

Words and Music by BENNY ANDERSSON,
BJÖRN ULVAEUS and STIG ANDERSON

# MY LOVE, MY LIFE

Words and Music by BENNY ANDERSSON
and BJÖRN ULVAEUS

# THE NAME OF THE GAME

Words and Music by BENNY ANDERSSON,
BJÖRN ULVAEUS and STIG ANDERSON

# SUPER TROUPER

Words and Music by BENNY ANDERSSON
and BJÖRN ULVAEUS

Su - per Trou - per beams are gon - na blind ___ me but I won't feel blue like I al - ways do, ___ 'cause some - where in the crowd ___ there's you.

# ONE OF US

Words and Music by BENNY ANDERSSON
and BJÖRN ULVAEUS

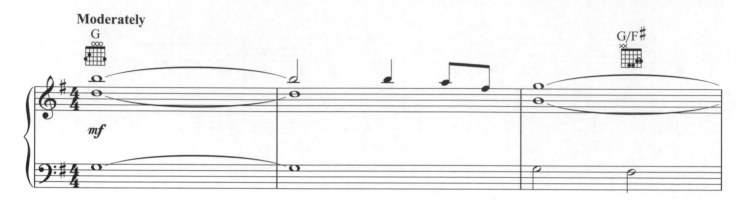

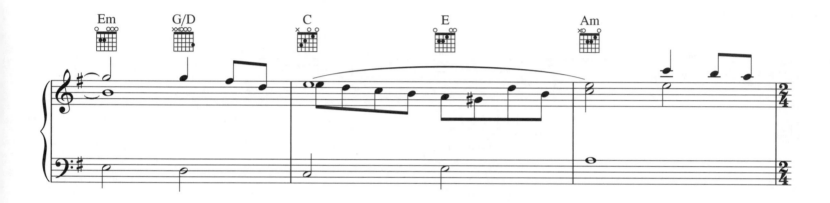

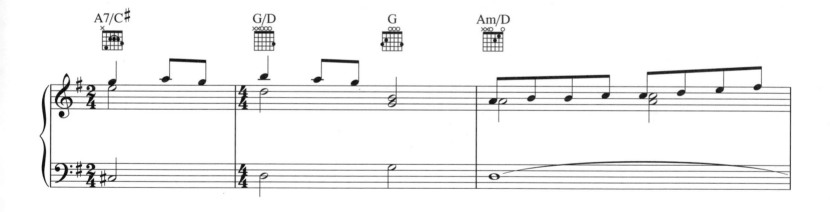

self, } feel - ing stu - pid, feel - ing small; wish - ing { he she } had nev - er left at all. __

Nev - er left __ at all.

Star - ing at the

Nev - er left ___ at all.

# WATERLOO

Words and Music by BENNY ANDERSSON,
BJÖRN ULVAEUS and STIG ANDERSON

# WHEN I KISSED THE TEACHER

Words and Music by BENNY ANDERSSON
and BJÖRN ULVAEUS

# WHY DID IT HAVE TO BE ME?

Words and Music by BENNY ANDERSSON
and BJÖRN ULVAEUS

Moderately

When you were lone - ly, you need - ed a man, _
Nights can be emp - ty, and nights can be cold, _

some-one to lean _ on; well, I un - der - stand. _
so you were look - ing for some one to hold. _

It's on - ly nat - 'ral, but
That's on - ly nat - 'ral, but

why did it have _ to be _____ me?
why did it have _ to be _____

Men are the toys __ in the game that you play. __ When you get tir - ed, you

throw them a - way. __ That's on - ly nat - 'ral, but why did it have __ to be _____

me?

Fall-ing in love ___ with a wom-an like you ___

hap-pens so quick - ly, there's noth-ing to do. ___ It's on - ly nat - 'ral, but

why did it have ___ to be _____ me?

I was so lone - some; I was blue. ___ I could-n't help ___ it, it

lieve me, it's bet - ter to for - get me.

(1st time only)

Repeat and Fade

Optional Ending